PIRATE QUEEN
OF IRELAND

THE ADVENTURES OF GRACE O'MALLEY

About the author
ANNE CHAMBERS is a best-selling biographer
who has received acclaim from critics and the reading public.
She has been shortlisted for the GPA and Hennessy literary awards,
and lectures extensively on the subjects of her books which
have been adapted for television and widely translated.

About the illustrator
DEIRDRE O'NEILL has a BA in Design from the Dublin Institute of
Technology. She has illustrated various other children's titles.

PIRATE QUEEN OF IRELAND

THE ADVENTURES OF GRACE O'MALLEY

ANNE CHAMBERS

Illustrations by Deirdre O'Neill

The Collins Press

PUBLISHED IN 2006 BY
The Collins Press
West Link Park
Doughcloyne
Wilton
Cork

Reprinted 2007, 2014

A Cataloguing-In-Publication data record for this book
is available from the British Library

ISBN-13: 978-1-84889-192-0

Typesetting: The Collins Press

Font: AGaramond, 13 point

Printed in Poland by Drukarnia Skleniarz

CONTENTS

INTRODUCTION

Seafarers are a special breed of people. Earning a living from the sea has always been a risky and dangerous business.

Even today, despite modern ship design and state-of-the-art satellite, computer and navigational equipment, a career at sea remains the choice of a brave few.

For those courageous enough to sail the oceans of the world, their names have been enshrined in history.

During the sixteenth century, Christopher Columbus, Ferdinand Magellan, Sir Francis Drake and Sir Walter Raleigh were among the most famous seafarers.

But during that time, nearer to home, lived another great seafarer whose story is less well known.

Her name was Grace O'Malley (Gráinne Ní Mháille), better known in Ireland as Granuaile.

And perhaps because she was a woman, Granuaile, unlike her male contemporaries, was not remembered in history. The sea was supposed to be for men only and seafaring was not thought a suitable career for a woman.

That is until Granuaile showed she was just as good a seafarer as any man and, without doubt, 'the most famous feminine sea-captain' of the sixteenth century.

For over 50 years she commanded a fleet of ships on the coasts of Ireland, Scotland and northern Spain. Like the other famous sailors of that time, she was a pirate as well as a sea trader.

But Granuaile was a powerful leader on land as well as sea. She commanded her own army, leading them personally into battle.

The English accused her of being 'the nurse to all rebellions' in Ireland and a 'chief director of thieves and murderers at sea'. But they also acknowledged her great ability and courage.

Granuaile was shrewd and calculating in her dealings with the English, especially with their queen, Elizabeth I. It was perhaps fitting that one day Granuaile and Elizabeth would come face to face.

The story of Granuaile is the story of one woman's courage and daring to be different in a time of great political unrest, and in one of the earth's most dangerous environments, the sea.

Chapter 1

THE WORLD OF GRANUAILE

But who was Granuaile? Where did she come from? How did she choose such a strange and dangerous career?

Granuaile was born around the year 1530. She was the only daughter of Dubhdara (Black Oak) O'Malley and his wife Margaret.

Her father was chieftain of the kingdom of Umhall, a small, remote territory bordering Clew Bay on the coast of County Mayo.

At this time Ireland was a very different country than to today. It did not have a government or a king. Instead, it was divided into about 40 independent 'kingdoms' or clans, like Umhall.

Each 'kingdom' was ruled by a Gaelic chieftain like Granuaile's father, or by a descendant of the Anglo-Normans, who had come to Ireland in the twelfth century, like Granuaile's neighbour, the Lower MacWilliam Bourke, chief of the Bourkes of Mayo.

Each ruler had his own army to protect his kingdom and his clan from attack by an enemy. To strengthen his own army, a chieftain often hired mercenary soldiers called the 'gallowglass' from Scotland.

The Irish chieftains ruled their territories by native Gaelic law, known as Brehon Law.

Brehon Law was different to English law in two important ways: how one became a chieftain and how one inherited property.

Chieftains and their successors, known as tanaiste, were elected by members of the clan. Unlike English nobility, they did not inherit their title automatically.

The chieftain had only a life interest in the lands he ruled on behalf of his clan. He could not pass them on to his eldest son, as the English noble did. On his death, the clan's lands reverted to the clan.

A chieftain measured his strength on the number of minor or client chiefs who paid him dues and provided him with troops when he went to war.

The client paid an agreed payment or tribute to the chief each year. These tributes ranged from a specific number of cattle, horses, bushels of wheat or jars of honey, to food and lodging for the chieftain and his family.

If the tribute was not paid on time, the chieftain could take it – and more – from his client by force.

In return, the chieftain was bound to protect his client and come to his aid in the event of his being attacked.

Granuaile's father was a client of the more powerful Lower MacWilliam Bourke of Mayo. Dubhdara's yearly tribute, however, amounted only to providing MacWilliam with a certain number of soldiers when he went to war.

The English had tried to conquer Ireland in the past. At the time of Granuaile's birth, however, they controlled only Dublin and a small area around it known as 'the Pale'.

The rest of the country was in the hands of the Gaelic chieftains and the descendants of the Anglo-Normans, many of whom, over time, had become 'more Irish than the Irish'.

But the English king, Henry VIII, wanted to rule all Ireland. He could not afford to send an army to conquer it by force. Instead in 1541 he tried to win over the Irish chieftains by a plan which he called 'surrender and re-grant'.

This plan meant that if a chieftain acknowledged Henry as king of Ireland and agreed to rule his lands by English rather than by Brehon Law, the king would re-grant him his lands and give him an English title.

Granuaile's father, Dubhdara, did not accept the king's offer but some of his neighbours did.

The Upper MacWilliam Burke, chieftain of the Burke clan of Galway, agreed and became the earl of Clanrickard. In Ulster, the O'Neill chieftain became the earl of Tyrone and in Munster O'Brien, the descendant of the great high king Brian Boru, was made earl of Thomond by the English king.

Just as the king intended, his policy divided the Irish clans. Some clans continued to elect their chieftain by Brehon Law. Those who lost out this way sought to gain the title by English law, with the help of the English, only too happy to have someone loyal to them in power.

While King Henry's surrender and re-grant policy took many years to take hold, it was the first step in England's plan to reconquer Ireland.

The Irish countryside in Granuaile's time also looked very different from today.

At this time much of the country was covered by great forests, woods and bogs. Wild animals such as wolves, wild boar and deer, roamed freely.

There were few roads and even fewer bridges by which to cross the rivers. This made travel by foot or horse very slow and difficult. It could take up to a month to get from the west coast to the east coast.

Ireland was famous for its cattle herds which were important to the economy. The more cattle a chieftain and his clan possessed the wealthier and more powerful they were.

There was little money in circulation. Instead people bought and sold by barter, that is, by exchanging goods.

Chieftains like Granuaile's father lived in stone-built castles or towers. The ruins of these towers can still be seen all around Ireland today. They were three or four storeys high and had a *bawn* or courtyard surrounded by high walls attached.

The chieftain and his family lived in the upper storey of the tower, which had a fireplace and narrow slit windows. The servants lived in the lower floors.

The walls of the castle were lime-washed and hung with antlers, skins and green-leafed branches. Rushes were strewn on the bare flag floor for comfort.

Dubhdara had a number of these castles situated around Clew Bay; at Cathair-na-Mart (Westport), Belclare, Murrisk, Carrowmore, Clare Island and Achill Island.

The chieftain's followers, or clansmen, lived with their families in small round cottages, made of wattle, earth or stone. The cottages clustered around the chieftain's castle for protection.

Neither the castles nor the cottages were very comfortable, having little heat or light and even less furniture.

People lived mainly out of doors, hunting, fishing and looking after the cattle herds and other domestic animals. They got up at sunrise and went to bed at sunset.

Like the people at the time, Granuaile and her family enjoyed a varied diet. They ate meat, fish, vegetables and a type of porridge made from oatmeal and milk, flavoured with butter.

They drank wine which was imported from France and Spain, buttermilk, home-made ale and whiskey. On special occasions they drank mead which was made from honey.

The main meal of the day was eaten in the evening.

Granuaile and her family sat down to eat at wooden tables on benches or stools. The food was placed on large wooden or pewter platters from which everyone helped themselves. Food was eaten with a knife and spoon since forks were at this time rare.

Falconry was a popular sport among the chieftains and their families and some of the best falconries were to be found among the mountains of Mayo and Galway.

Deer hunting on horseback with Irish wolfhounds and hunting

The young Granuaile.

9

wild boar were other popular outdoor pursuits of the time.

Travelling musicians and storytellers sometimes entertained Granuaile and her family in their castle. The harp and bagpipes were among the musical instruments then played.

These musicians and storytellers also brought news and gossip from other parts of the country. Because there was no postal system or newspapers, this was the only way people could find out what was happening outside their own area.

Chess, dice and cards were popular pastimes.

Granuaile became known as a shrewd gambler and was often called 'Grainne na gCearbach' (Grace of the Gamblers).

Chapter 2

CHILD OF THE SEA

Granuaile was born into a clan that was different from other Gaelic clans in one special way.

For hundreds of years, the O'Malleys had been sailing their ships around the coast of Ireland and farther afield to Scotland and northern Spain, trading, fishing and plundering.

The Gaelic poets called them 'the lions of the green sea'.

Granuaile's father commanded the O'Malley fleet. He was a strong and powerful chieftain.

Dubhdara dressed in the traditional *léine*, a linen shirt, pleated at the waist, tight-fitting woollen trousers and square-toed leather shoes. Over his *léine* he wore a sleeveless leather jerkin. When it was cold he wrapped himself in a large woollen *brat* or cloak which had a deep fringe around the neck.

Women of Granuaile's time wore a linen dress under a sleeveless light woollen tunic reaching to the ground. Women also wore a *brat*.

In summer the clan's cattle herds were driven up to the pastures high on the mountain and hillsides to graze. The chieftain, his followers and their families lived in small huts on the uplands and looked after the herds.

This custom known as 'booleying' was called after the type of houses, i.e.'booley', in which the people lived. It was a very ancient custom which had been in practice for centuries.

More than anything else Granuaile wanted to go to sea with her father. The sea was in her blood. But the sea was thought to be too dangerous and certainly no place for a girl, especially a chieftain's daughter.

There is a story that Granuaile cut her hair, dressed up in boy's clothes, stowed away on her father's ship and soon learned to be as good a sailor as her father. But one way or another, Granuaile could not be kept away from the sea.

She had much to learn. She had to become an expert judge of the tides, the currents and the many moods of the sea; to become, as the poet wrote of her clan, a 'prophet of the weather'. She had to know when it was safe to sail and when to stay ashore.

She also had to learn all about the ships she sailed; about canvas, ropes, ballast and anchors; to know how to navigate by the stars and by compass; to steer her ship safely around rocks, shallows and underwater reefs.

Granuaile also learned about the business her father conducted by sea: how to trade, fish, pilot and plunder.

In summer the O'Malley clan fished for herring in the rich waters off Clare Island and Achill. The herring was then salted and packed in wooden barrels.

Together with wool, cattle hides, the skins of pine marten, rabbit and fox, tallow (made from the lard of cattle and which was used for making candles) and butter, the herring was transported in the O'Malley's ships to Spain.

The ships returned from Spain with cargoes of salt, wine, iron, weapons and alum, a substance used for dying clothes, as well as cloth, such as cambric and damask, and Spanish fashions and furnishings – for those who could afford them.

Dubhdara had the biggest fleet of ships in Ireland. As well as smaller boats, like coracles and curraghs, he had a number of larger ships called galleys.

Galleys were made of wooden planks which overlapped each other to make the ship water-tight. They had a small deck to the stern. They were powered by a triangular sail, known as a lateen sail. They were also rowed by as many as 30 oarsmen. The O'Malley galleys could accommodate up to 100 men in each and they were a fast and agile vessel in the water.

As well as trading the clan produce, the O'Malleys were often involved in the plunder and piracy of other ships, especially merchant ships on their way from England and the continent to the nearby town of Galway.

Wealthy merchants controlled the trade of Galway city. If Granuaile's clan wanted to sell their goods there, the merchants made them pay high taxes. This meant that they made little profit. That is why the O'Malleys traded their goods in their own ships directly to Spain instead.

To get their own back on the merchants, the O'Malleys made the Galway ships pay taxes, called tolls, to sail through O'Malley waters off the west coast.

If the ship's captain refused to pay, then the O'Malleys simply took some of the ship's cargo instead. The slow-moving merchant ships were no match for their faster galleys.

At this time there were no accurate maps of Ireland. The west coast, with its rocky headlands and underwater reefs, was much feared by foreign sea captains.

The O'Malleys were hired to pilot foreign ships and bring them safely along the dangerous coastline.

The O'Malley galleys and crews were also hired by other chieftains to bring in the mercenary soldiers, the gallowglass, from Scotland.

Granuaile's father issued licences to Spanish and English fishermen to fish in the rich waters under his control off Clew Bay.

As Granuaile grew up, she could see how important the sea was to her family. It provided them with an income.

But she also realised that as long as they had their own ships and controlled their sea territory off the west coast, the sea also made them independent and free.

It was a lesson she would never forget.

Chapter 3

THE COCK AND THE HEN

When she was fifteen years old, Granuaile's seafaring life came to a sudden end. Her parents decided it was time for her to marry. But she could not choose her own husband.

Her marriage was an important event, not only for her parents, but for the entire O'Malley clan. A marriage between two clans would help to unite them in times of trouble.

Her father searched for a suitable partner for her from among the eligible sons of other chieftains. He chose Donal O'Flaherty, known by his nickname, Donal-an-Chogaidh, Donal-of-the Battles.

At the time of his marriage to Granuaile, Donal was chieftain of Ballinahinch, a territory on the west coast of Galway, near Slyne Head.

He was also the elected tanaiste, and would eventually become senior chieftain of all Iar-Chonnacht, that is present-day Connemara.

The match was thought to be a good one for Granuaile. Donal was a strong chieftain and his future political prospects looked good.

From Granuaile's point of view, the fact that her husband's castle was on the coast and that he also owned some ships helped ease the pain of being parted from her family and from the sea.

On her marriage, her father gave Granuaile a large *spréidh* or dowry. This consisted of a number of cattle and sheep, as well as household linen, furnishings and utensils for her new home.

Granuaile's dowry was protected by legal safeguards, agreed by her father and her in-laws. This ensured that, in the event of Donal's death, or if they became divorced, she would receive part of her husband's property for her lifetime, equivalent to the amount of her dowry.

Granuaile and Donal lived in Bunowen Castle. It was much like the castles she grew up in at home and it also looked out onto the sea. From the window to the east she could see the towering peaks of the Twelve Bens and knew that beyond them was her home in Umhall.

Granuaile settled into her new home. Over time she and Donal had two sons, Owen and Murrough, and a daughter called Margaret, named after Granuaile's mother.

As the wife of a chieftain Granuaile was expected to manage his castle and servants, and organise food and lodging for his guests and fellow chieftains when they visited.

Everything seemed to indicate a prosperous and happy life for Granuaile.

But Donal had not earned his nickname for nothing. He was a reckless and warlike chieftain. He was constantly feuding with his neighbouring clans. This brought hardship to his own clan, whose lands, crops and herds were often destroyed in revenge attacks by Donal's enemies.

That is why his clansmen began to look to Granuaile to provide for and protect them. She did it in the way she knew best – by sea.

The merchants of Galway had barred the O'Flahertys from entering the city. Over the western gate the citizens of the town had written: 'From the Ferocious O'Flahertys, Good Lord Deliver Us.'

Granuaile led her husband's followers on attacks on ships sailing into Galway, taking tolls for safe passage.

In her faster galley, Granuaile and her men lay in wait for the heavily-laden merchant ship. If the captain refused to pay, then Granuaile took part of his cargo instead. Then, as quickly as they appeared, Granuaile and her men disappeared, lost in the maze of the coastal inlets and islands off the coast of Connemara. With no accurate map, the captain knew he dare not follow her.

Soon the name of Granuaile became known and feared all along the west coast.

The Mayor and Corporation of Galway complained about her to

the English Government in Dublin. But there was little they could do to stop her.

In 1558 England got a new ruler, Henry VIII's daughter, Elizabeth.

Like her father, Elizabeth could not afford to conquer Ireland by force. Instead, she tried to use the feuding between the Irish chieftains to her advantage. Divide and conquer became her policy as she began to replace troublesome chieftains with those who promised to be loyal to her.

Elizabeth's policy soon affected Granuaile and her husband.

When the senior chieftain of Iar-Chonnact died, Granuaile's husband, as his tanaiste, should have succeeded him. But Elizabeth chose another O'Flaherty. He had no right by Gaelic law to become the chieftain but he had promised to rule Iar-Chonnact by English law.

This was a big set-back for Granuaile and her husband. But instead of defending his rights from the English, Donal was fighting with his neighbours the Joyces over the ownership of a castle in Lough Corrib, known as Cock's Castle.

The castle changed hands many times in the dispute. Eventually Donal was killed while defending it from an attack by the Joyces.

The Joyces thought the castle was theirs at last, but they had not thought about Granuaile.

Leading her husband's clansmen, she defended Cock's Castle so bravely that it was at once renamed 'Hen's Castle' in her honour. That is the name it still has today.

This was not the only time Granuaile was forced to defend Hen's Castle. The Galway merchants sent an army to besiege her there. They thought they had cornered the infamous pirate leader at last.

With food supplies running low, Granuaile had to think of some way of getting the soldiers away from the castle walls. She ordered her men to strip the lead roof, melt it down and pour the hot liquid over the ramparts, on to the soldiers beneath. The soldiers quickly retreated.

But despite her bravery and success as a leader, Granuaile could not become chieftain in her husband's place. Brehon Law did not permit women to be chieftains. Her husband's cousin was elected chieftain instead.

Her sons, now young men, would have to wait their turn to put themselves forward for election as chieftain.

With nothing to hold her in Ballinahinch, Grace returned home to Umhall in 1562. Some of the O'Flaherty clansmen chose to follow her.

Chapter 4

THE PIRATE QUEEN

As a widow, Granuaile had another reason for returning to Umhall.

If Brehon Law did not allow a woman to be elected chieftain, unlike English law, it did permit women to own land and property. And Granuaile had inherited land in Umhall from her mother.

On her return, since her father was growing old, she also took over control of the O'Malley fleet.

She established her base on Clare Island. The island was perfectly situated at the mouth of Clew Bay. The castle gave her a clear view of the bay, and its concealed position meant it could not be seen by passing ships, which gave Granuaile the advantage of a surprise attack.

From Donegal to Waterford, news of this woman seafarer and pirate grew. The MacSweeneys of Lough Swilly, the islanders of Inishbofin and the Aran Islands, the inhabitants of Renvyle Castle in Connemara, the O'Loughlin chief of the Burren of Clare, all felt the brunt of her raids.

In Dublin and London, stories about her reached the English

government who named her 'the most notorious woman in all the coasts of Ireland'.

What kind of a woman, people whispered, would lead such a dangerous and unfeminine life? Women were supposed to stay at home and look after their husband and family, not go careering on the seas trading and plundering. This woman has 'overstepped the part of womanhood', one English official complained about her.

But Granuaile was no ordinary woman. Above all else she was an O'Malley. Seafaring, including plunder, was in her blood.

Her bravery and success made men from other clans in Connaught want to join her. Soon she had a private army of over 200 men.

Granuaile must have been a very special person for these hardy clansmen from different clans to accept her as their leader. And she was. She had charisma and courage.

Granuaile led her men herself in battle, by land and sea. She endured the same dangers and hardships. Her daring is remembered in the lines of a poem:

> No braver seaman took a deck in hurricane or squall
> Since Grace O'Malley battered down old Curraith Castle's walls.

Most of all, Granuaile was an expert seafarer. Her men trusted her and this created a special bond between them.

She was proud of the loyalty of her men and once said that she would 'rather have a ship full of MacNallys and Conroys than a ship full of gold'.

She could also be ruthless and especially so when avenging a wrong done to her.

During her time on Clare Island, in the teeth of a gale, she bravely rescued a young man called Hugh de Lacy, whose ship had foundered on rocks on Achill Island.

She and Hugh fell deeply in love but their happiness was short-lived. Hugh was soon murdered by a neighbouring clan, the MacMahons, from Doona Castle in Erris.

After mourning Hugh, Granuaile bided her time to avenge his death.

When the MacMahons came on a pilgrimage to the holy island of Caher, near Clare Island, she swooped like an eagle.

She captured their boats and killed those responsible for Hugh's murder. Then she sailed to Doona and took the MacMahon's castle for herself.

Her enemies knew that Granuaile was someone not to be crossed.

Chapter 5

KIDNAPPED

It was to avenge a slight made to her that Granuaile's name is remembered in a very special way for over 400 years in a part of Ireland far from Clare Island.

While returning from a trading voyage in 1575, Granuaile was forced to land at Howth near Dublin. Howth was then part of the English-controlled Pale.

While her ship was being repaired and fitted out for the voyage back to Clew Bay, Granuaile came ashore.

With a few of her men she walked up from the harbour towards Howth Castle. This was the residence of the Lord of Howth, Christopher St Lawrence. Granauile decided to pay him a visit.

She knocked loudly on the castle door. A servant demanded to know what she wanted. Granuaile told him she sought the owner's hospitality. The servant returned and rudely told her that the Lord of Howth said he was at his dinner and would not be disturbed.

Granuaile was furious. If St Lawrence had visited her in her castle in Mayo she would have been obliged by the rules of Gaelic

Granuaile and her men approach Howth Castle.

25

hospitality to give him food and shelter. Instead, all she had received at his castle was an insult.

Returning to her ship, she met a young boy walking along the beach. She stopped to talk to him and found out he was the grandson and heir of the Lord of Howth.

She resolved to teach his inhospitable grandfather a lesson he would never forget.

She invited the boy on board her ship and immediately set sail for Clew Bay.

When news was brought to the Lord of Howth that his grandson and heir had been 'kidnapped' by a notorious pirate from the west of Ireland, he was frantic with worry.

Taking some gold and silver with him to pay a ransom, he set off on horseback on the long, difficult journey across Ireland.

Meanwhile Granuaile had returned to Clare Island. She took good care that her young captive would come to no harm.

Eventually the Lord of Howth arrived in Umhall. He begged Granuaile to name any ransom she wished for the safe return of his heir.

Scorning his offer of gold and silver, Granuaile's ransom demand took the nobleman by surprise.

She made him promise that the door of Howth Castle would never be closed and that every time he sat down at his table to dine, an extra place would be set at his table for anyone seeking his hospitality.

Surprised and relieved, the Lord of Howth promised to carry out Granuaile's wishes. Before he left with his grandson the nobleman gave her a ring to seal their bargain. The ring was kept in the O'Malley family for many generations.

In Howth today, Granuaile's visit is still remembered. Many roads in the village bear her name.

In the castle, which is owned by the descendants of the same Lord of Howth, her ransom demands are faithfully carried out by the family to this very day.

When the owner of Howth Castle sits down to dinner, he always has an extra place set at his table to honour the promise his ancestor made 400 years ago to Granuaile.

Chapter 6

RICHARD-IN-IRON

While Granuaile continued to build her reputation and her business, political events were happening elsewhere that would soon affect her life and that of her country.

In Europe the old Catholic and new Protestant religions were coming into conflict.

The Catholics looked to King Philip II of Spain for protection while the Protestants turned to Queen Elizabeth I of England.

As well as religion, another problem had arisen between Spain and England.

English pirates, like Sir Francis Drake, with the blessing of Queen Elizabeth, regularly attacked King Philip's treasure ships as they returned to Spain from the Americas full of silver and gold.

King Philip began to plot revenge on Elizabeth.

Elizabeth feared the king might use Ireland as a back door to attack England. She realised that if she wanted to continue to rule England, she would have to control Ireland as well.

The sixteenth century was the age of exploration and discovery. There was a hunger in Europe for new lands and new sources of wealth.

For English speculators and adventurers, Ireland was nearer to home than the faraway Americas. If the feuding Gaelic chiefs could be overcome, their fertile lands would make a great prize.

In 1565 the idea of colonisation was introduced in England as a way to both conquer Ireland and satisfy this desire for land.

It was proposed to send loyal Englishmen to Ireland to settle on Irish-owned lands. The idea was greeted with great enthusiasm in England.

Armed with ancient deeds, most of them flawed, many going back to the Norman invasion of the twelfth century, which laid claim to the lands of Gaelic chieftains, scores of English adventurers arrived, firstly in Munster.

The Gaelic chieftains and lords of Munster tried to protect their lands by whatever means they could: some did it by force, others by converting to English law.

To protect the English colonists and to extend its rule outside of the Pale, the English appointed two governors to rule Munster and Connaught. With these governors came English judges, sheriffs and tax collectors.

The Elizabethan conquest of Ireland had started in earnest.

While Mayo, as yet, was not directly affected by these political developments, Granuaile could see that strength meant power. She decided it was time to look for an ally.

She chose Richard-in-Iron, chieftain of the Bourkes of Burrishoole and Carra. He was a strong if, at times, headstrong chieftain on land – an ideal mate for Granuaile whose power was by sea.

Richard had a number of castles on the north side of Clew Bay, including the seaside castle of Carraigahowley, which had a fine sheltered harbour.

It was thought that Richard got his nickname from a suit of old-fashioned armour he wore. It is more likely, however, that his nickname came from the iron mines on his land.

In 1566 Granuaile and Richard got married. Granuaile married her second husband on her own terms. She agreed to become his wife for 'one year certain', meaning that if she wanted to leave the marriage she was free to do so after one year.

It was said that when the year was up Granuaile divorced her husband. She locked him out of his castle of Carraigahowley, installed herself with her followers there, and anchored her ships in his fine harbour.

It was also said that she kept the mooring rope of her favourite galley tied to her bedpost in Carraigahowley, in case Richard or anyone else tried to steal it from her while she was asleep.

Granuaile and Richard patched up their differences although Granuaile 'wore the trousers' in her marriage to Richard. But together they made a formidable couple. He was powerful by land; she was powerful by sea.

This made the English very wary of crossing swords with them.

Chapter 7

TOBY-OF-THE-SHIPS

In 1567, a son was born to Granuaile and Richard, whom they named Theobald.

He became better known in history as Tibóid-na-Long (Toby-of-the-Ships), a suitable name given how and where he was born.

Granuaile was returning from a long trading voyage when she went into labour. Tibóid was born on board her ship in the midst of a violent storm.

In the lull that followed, as she was nursing her new-born baby, her ship was attacked by North African pirates, known as 'corsairs'.

The corsairs were much feared everywhere. They often took women and children prisoners and brought them back to North Africa as slaves.

At this time, North African corsairs had attacked many coastal villages, particularly on the south coast of Ireland.

The corsairs managed to board Granuaile's galley and a battle raged on deck.

Without Granuaile to lead them, her crew were all but defeated. Her captain hurried below and begged Granuaile to come up on deck so that her presence might rally her men.

Tired after the birth of her son and furious that her men could not beat off the corsairs without her, she gave out to them saying, 'May you be seven times worse off this day next year for not being able to do without me for one day'.

Coming up on deck, Granuaile rallied her men. The corsairs could not believe their eyes when they saw a woman in command.

With sword in hand, she attacked them with such ferocity that they beat a hasty retreat, leaving many of their number dead behind them.

With such a start in life, it is little wonder that, like his mother, Tibóid became an accomplished seafarer. Like his father though, he was also skilled in warfare.

A poet described him as having 'hawk-like blue eyes ... golden-yellow hair ... and ruddy cheeks'.

At six years old his parents fostered him with a neighbouring chieftain. Fosterage was a Gaelic custom. It was considered a mark of honour to be the fosterer of the son of a greater chieftain. It also bound both clans closer together in both peace and war.

Granuaile fighting the Corsairs.

In his foster home Tibóid received all the care, affection and training that his foster parents gave their own children.

As a future chieftain, from boyhood Tibóid was trained to use weapons such as the sword, lance, javelin and dart, both on foot and on horseback.

Later as a youth he learned all about sea-faring from his mother. He also inherited her keen and able mind which he used to good effect later in negotiating with the English.

Unlike most of his fellow countrymen, Tibóid was also able to speak and write both in Irish and English, and some of his letters are preserved in the English State Papers of the time.

Chapter 8

'A MOST FAMOUS FEMININE SEA CAPTAIN'

England continued to extend its rule into areas of Ireland which up until then were controlled by the Gaelic chieftains and lords.

It was not long before it began to affect Granuaile and her family.

In 1571, her husband, Richard-in-Iron, was elected tanaiste to succeed Shane Bourke, the MacWilliam of Mayo, chief of all the Bourkes.

To become the MacWilliam was the ambition of every Bourke chief in Mayo. The position brought great power, lands and wealth. Richard and Granuaile's future seemed bright.

In 1576 Queen Elizabeth's representative in Ireland, the lord deputy, Sir Henry Sidney, came with an army into Connaught. The lord deputy ordered the chieftains who had not yet accepted English rule to appear before him in Galway.

The MacWilliam of Mayo and his tanaiste, Richard-in-Iron, refused. They wanted no interference in the way they ruled their lands.

The lord deputy did not have an army big enough to attack

MacWilliam and Richard. He had to think of another way to make them submit. He bribed their gallowglass away from them and so reduced the strength of their army.

Fearing that the English would attack his lands and overpower him, MacWilliam submitted to the lord deputy. He promised he would rule Mayo in future by English law and pay taxes to the Queen.

Granuaile heard of this disturbing development. Experience had taught her that, by English law, MacWilliam's nearest male relation would now succeed him when he died, instead of Richard, his tanaiste.

Granuaile vowed that her second husband would not be deprived of his rights, as her first husband had been.

She decided to let the English lord deputy see for himself that she and Richard were a force to be reckoned with – that if Richard did not become the MacWilliam, the English would have a fight on their hands.

When Sir Henry Sidney returned to Galway in 1577, he met Granuaile and, as she intended, he was impressed.

This is how Sidney reported their meeting.

There came to me a most famous feminine sea captain, called Grany I Mallye ... with three galleys and 200 fighting men ... She brought with her her husband ... nicknamed Richard-in-Iron. This was the most notorious woman in all the coasts of Ireland.

Sir Henry Sidney's son, Philip, who at that time was one of the most famous English poets of the day, also met and spoke with Granuaile. He had come to Ireland to visit his father and had accompanied him on his visit to Galway.

Granuaile's plan worked. The English lord deputy was sufficiently impressed to realise that with her army and ships she would make a better friend than an enemy.

He seemed less impressed with Richard-in-Iron, however, whom, as he wrote to the English court, seemed to play second fiddle to his wife.

She brought with her her husband, for she was as well by sea as by land well more than Mrs Mate with him ...

Since the lord deputy had no ships of his own, he asked Granuaile if she would bring him in her galley for a trip around Galway Bay so that he might examine the defences of the city from the sea.

Granuaile agreed to his request. But, business being business, she made the lord deputy pay his fare.

Chapter 9

CAPTURE AND IMPRISONMENT

Satisfied that she had made the English realise the extent of her power, Granuaile returned to her usual seafaring trade.

She sailed south to plunder the rich lands of the earl of Desmond in Munster, the most powerful lord in Ireland.

This time, however, the mission did not work out quite as planned. She and some of her men were captured.

She was brought before the earl at his great castle at Askeaton in County Limerick. Desmond threw her into his dungeons where she remained for almost a year.

Imprisonment was a terrible fate to befall anyone but especially Granuaile. Since childhood she had been used to the freedom of the sea and had always been independent.

Now, like a wild animal, she was held captive, with execution her likely fate. Time ebbed slowly. Day after day she prowled up and down her narrow cell.

But her captor had his own problems. The English feared the earl's

Granuaile imprisoned in Dublin Castle.

power and were envious of his vast estates and castles. They wanted to get their hands on his land to give to English colonists.

As well as that, England's chief enemy Spain, together with the Pope, was trying to persuade Desmond to lead a Catholic rebellion in Ireland against the Protestant queen of England.

The English were watching Desmond closely. At the time of Granuaile's capture, he played a waiting game. He was trying to make up his mind whether to join forces with Spain against England or remain as he was.

He desperately needed something to keep the English at arm's length. Granuaile provided him with the answer to his problem.

When the English president of Munster, Sir William Drury, and his army arrived before the walls of Askeaton Castle, Desmond produced Granuaile, as proof of his 'loyalty' to the English queen.

Drury was suitably impressed. He wrote to his superiors in London about his famous prisoner. He accused Granuaile of being 'a chief commander of thieves and murderers at sea' and described her as 'a woman who had impudently passed the part of womanhood', in other words, that she had the nerve to compete with men.

While he completed his tour of Munster, Drury had Granuaile imprisoned in Limerick gaol.

From Limerick she was taken in chains and brought across the country to Dublin Castle, where the most important political prisoners were kept.

By now she had been in prison for eighteen months. Accused of plunder, piracy and treason, execution was staring her in the face.

But somehow she managed to secure her freedom. In early 1579 she was released from Dublin Castle. How she managed to get free is a mystery.

As rumours of Desmond's intrigue with Spain increased, perhaps the English did not consider plundering the lands of a suspected traitor was such a crime any more.

Chapter 10

UNDER SIEGE

On her release from prison, Granuaile hurried back to Umhall. Her family and her men could hardly believe their eyes when they saw her. She had been gone for so long they thought she had been executed. Few prisoners ever got free from Dublin Castle. There was great joy and much celebration at her return.

But news of the return of the famous pirate was not welcomed everywhere. When the merchants of Galway heard of it, they knew their ships would have to pay tolls again. They decided to stop Granuaile before she could get started.

They paid for an army, commanded by Captain Martin from Galway, to sail into Clew Bay. They besieged Granuaile in her castle of Carraigahowley.

Granuaile was taken by surprise. Showing great bravery, she held out for 27 days before turning the tables on the besiegers and chasing them out of Clew Bay and right back to Galway.

In November 1579, her former gaoler, the earl of Desmond, finally made up his mind and rebelled. With a huge army, comprised of many of his client lords and chiefs in Munster, he decided to take on the English.

Queen Elizabeth had him proclaimed a traitor. This meant that if he was captured or killed, his huge estate would be forfeited to her.

The English army attacked his territory and the Desmond rebellion, which was to last for four years, began.

Desmond asked for help from the Connaught chieftains. Granuaile had no reason to help her former captor but her husband, Richard-in-Iron, set out with his army for Munster.

Granuaile was furious with her husband. Desmond's rebellion against the English in Munster had nothing to do with them. Her only concern was to protect and provide for her family and her followers.

She also realised that her husband's action would serve only to bring the English army into Umhall.

Granuaile was proved right. In 1580 the English governor of Connaught, Sir Nicholas Malby, drove Richard and his army from Munster, through Galway, back into Mayo, burning and looting everything in his path.

When his gallowglass deserted him, Richard fled to Granuaile for help.

Malby pursued Richard to the shores of Clew Bay. Richard escaped to one of the islands in the bay, leaving Granuaile to deal with Malby.

Granuaile opened negotiations with the governor. With great skill and cunning, she eventually succeeded in achieving good terms and a pardon for her husband.

More importantly, she got the English troops out of her territory.

Chapter 11

'NO SMALL LADY'

In November 1580, the MacWilliam of Mayo died. By Gaelic law, as his tanaiste, Richard-in-Iron should have succeeded him. But since the MacWilliam had accepted English law, his title and lands would instead be inherited by his next male heir, his brother.

Granuaile and Richard were having none of it. They joined their forces to fight for their rights.

Granuaile's ships brought in the gallowglass from Scotland. The other clans in Mayo came out to support them.

The English army was still fighting the earl of Desmond in Munster and was already stretched to its limit. The English knew they stood little chance against the combined power of Granuaile, Richard and their allies in Connaught. They agreed to talk.

Both sides met in Mayo and a deal was struck. Richard was to become the MacWilliam. The previous MacWilliam's brother was to become his tanaiste.

Richard was to have the lands, amounting to 7,000 acres, and the castles that went with the title. He was to receive all the payments which the MacWilliam usually received by Brehon custom from his client chiefs in Mayo.

In return, Richard promised to rule his lordship by English law and to pay 50 cows to the English government each year in tax.

To put an English gloss on his Gaelic title of MacWilliam, the Queen knighted him as 'Sir Richard Bourke'.

The ceremony was carried out by the governor of Connaught in Galway. 'The MacWilliam ... and many gentlemen and their wives are here, among them Grace O'Malley who thinks herself to be no small Lady,' the Governor reported back to England.

So Granuaile became Lady Bourke, the wife of the most powerful chieftain in Connaught, as well as a chieftain in her own right.

But no one dared call her anything but Granuaile.

Granuaile and Richard moved with their son, Tibóid, away from Clew Bay, inland to Lough Mask Castle, the principal residence of the MacWilliam. Tibóid was fostered nearby with a clan called MacEvilly.

Granuaile and her husband were now at the height of their power. Every clan in Mayo paid them homage, as well as substantial dues in money, cattle, horses, sheep, produce and weapons, as was the Gaelic custom.

Granuaile with her husband, Sir Richard Bourke, and clansmen.

When the English tried to force them to pay the tax they had agreed to, Granuaile and her army sent the tax collector and his armed guard packing. The tax collector feared for his life and reported that Granuaile had threatened to kill him.

For two years Richard and Granuaile ruled undisputed in Mayo. They were a powerful and wealthy couple.

In April 1583, however, Richard suddenly died. Granuaile was a widow once more.

Her second marriage, despite its ups and downs, had been a marriage of equals. Despite their differences, Granuaile and Richard were a well-suited pair. Both were brave but Granuaile was the cleverer.

On the death of her husband, Granuaile gathered together all her followers. With her own herds, which by then numbered 1,000 head of cattle and horses, she returned to Umhall.

She settled in her husband's castle of Carraigahowley, which she took in place of her dowry. Soon she was back to the life she loved best – the sea.

Granuaile was now 53 years of age. She seemed likely to live out her remaining years in comfort in her castle near the sea. But fate had other things in store for her.

Chapter 12

SIR RICHARD BINGHAM

Up to now Granuaile, by her sheer courage and ability, had managed to keep the English away from her territory. She was still a powerful leader by land and sea. She had her own ships, her own army, a fortune in cattle and horses, and her castle.

But the arrival of Sir Richard Bingham as governor of Connaught in 1584 spelled the beginning of the end, not only for Granuaile, but for her native Gaelic world.

Up to now the English had been content to try and persuade the chieftains in Connaught to accept English law by peaceful means.

But when England's enemy Spain began to support the Gaelic chiefs in their struggle against England – as they had done with the earl of Desmond in Munster – Queen Elizabeth decided that the time had come to conquer Ireland once and for all.

The fate of the once-powerful earl of Desmond was a terrible warning and example to other chiefs of Elizabeth's determination.

His great castle of Askeaton was gutted, his lands burned and pillaged. For two years the earl was hunted from one part of his lordship to the other, forced to live like a wild animal in the forests of Munster.

When eventually he was captured, Desmond's head was sent to the Queen in England. She had it put on a spike outside the Tower of London, where the earl's young son and heir was imprisoned.

Because the earl had died in rebellion, by English law, his huge estates were confiscated to the Crown. They were divided among new English planters and among the English soldiers who had fought against him.

Famous Englishmen like Sir Walter Raleigh and the poet Edmund Spenser were granted some of Desmond's lands and castles, while the earl's only son got nothing.

Now it was the turn of Granuaile and her neighbours in Mayo to either accept English law or have their property and lands taken from them also.

And Sir Richard Bingham was just the man to do it.

Bingham was a military man. His opinion was that 'the Irish would never be tamed by words but with swords'. Very soon he began to put that opinion into practice.

One of his first acts as governor was to hang 70 people in Galway. He next hit at the Bourkes in Mayo and hanged the MacWilliam's tanaiste, Edmund Bourke, and confiscated his lands.

The Mayo chieftains, including Granuaile and her family, rose in rebellion to protect their lands and property.

The rebellion spread into the territory of Granuaile's sons, Owen and Murrough O'Flaherty, in Iar-Chonnacht.

Captain John Bingham, the governor's brother, seized Granuaile's eldest son Owen and had him killed while he was in his custody.

Granuaile was devastated by the murder of her eldest son. She vowed vengeance on the English governor. Her ships brought in the gallowglass from Scotland to help the rebellion.

But very soon she herself was captured by Captain John Bingham, who trapped her near her castle of Carraigahowley.

Granuaile later told Queen Elizabeth what had happened to her. 'She was apprehended and tied with a rope. Both she and her followers were spoiled [robbed] of their cattle and she was brought to Sir Richard.'

Bingham was delighted to capture such an important rebel leader. He executed two of her nephews who had been taken with her and threw Granuaile into prison.

Knowing that she was one of the principal leaders of the rebellion and that she had brought the gallowglass from Scotland into Connaught, Bingham vowed to make an example of Granuaile.

He ordered a new gallows to be specially built on which to hang her publicly as a deterrent to others. Granuaile faced the end bravely.

While she awaited her fate, her daughter's husband, Richard Bourke, chieftain of Achill, tricked Bingham into accepting him as a hostage in her place. Once Granuaile was free, Richard Bourke also escaped Bingham's clutches by pretending to become a royal subject of the Queen.

Granuaile immediately set sail in her ships to Scotland to hire more gallowglass.

On her voyage north a violent storm overtook her. Her ships were so battered and broken, she was forced to put ashore for repairs in Ulster.

There she visited two of the most powerful chieftains in the country, O'Neill and O'Donnell. They had contacts with the Spanish court. They told her about the exciting news they had heard – that Spain was planning an invasion of England.

But her family and followers in Mayo were Granuaile's immediate concern. If she returned to Mayo though, Bingham would have her executed. She thought of a plan.

She knew there was little love lost between the new lord deputy in Dublin, Sir John Perrot, and Bingham. So she travelled to Dublin and put her case to the lord deputy.

Perrot listened sympathetically to her litany of complaints against Bingham.

She asked Perrot for a pardon for herself and the members of her family whom Bingham had accused of being rebels. Perrot agreed and promised he would do his best to have Bingham removed from office.

Armed with a Royal Pardon, Granuaile knew Bingham could not now harm her or her family.

By the time she got back to Mayo, she found that the rebellion was over. The land was ruined and the people exhausted from the fighting.

But Perrot kept his word and Bingham was removed from Connaught and transferred to Flanders.

The whole of Connaught breathed a sigh of relief and hoped they would never set eyes on him again.

Free once more to return to her business by sea, Granuaile made up for lost time.

Chapter 13

THE SPANISH ARMADA

On 29 July 1588, the 130 ships of the Spanish Armada were sighted off the south coast of England. Fiery beacons, from hilltop to hilltop, conveyed the terrifying news across England.

The long-feared Spanish invasion was at hand.

By sending small, unmanned fireships in among the bigger Spanish vessels, the English navy managed to scatter the great ships of the Armada in the English Channel before they could land.

Then a great storm arose and drove the Spanish ships northwards towards Scotland. England was saved.

There was nothing for the Armada to do but head home to Spain.

On the way, the wind and the strong currents drove the ships too close to the dangerous north and west coasts of Ireland.

The Spanish captains had no accurate map of the Irish coast. Many of the ships crashed on to the rocky headlands or went aground in the shallows.

The Spanish Armada.

Thousands of Spanish sailors and soldiers were drowned. Those who managed to scramble ashore received a mixed welcome from the Irish.

Few of the ordinary people in Ireland knew much about the Armada. When the great ships crashed onto the rocks and split asunder, the people along the coast thought only of the treasure they could salvage from the wreck.

They were also fearful of English reprisals if they helped the survivors.

Many of the Spanish castaways were killed, others were stripped of their belongings and left to fend for themselves.

Some Irish chieftains, like O'Neill and O'Rourke in Ulster, however, did save hundreds of survivors and eventually got them safe passage back to Spain.

Many of the Spanish ships were wrecked on the coast of Connaught. Two went aground in Clew Bay.

The English government feared that the Spanish would join forces with the Gaelic clans, especially Granuaile and her family. Some of them did.

The English made it a crime punishable by death to shelter the Spanish. Sir Richard Bingham was sent back to Connaught to put that order into effect and to round up the remaining survivors.

Chapter 14

'NURSE TO ALL REBELLIONS'

Bingham made up for lost time. On his arrival he immediately sent an army to search the lands of Granuaile and her family.

He also ordered that the property of any chieftain found sheltering the Spaniards was to be destroyed and their land confiscated.

The army, under the command of the sheriff of Mayo, John Browne, reached Granuaile's castle in February 1589. Granuaile's army and that of her son-in-law, Richard Bourke, barred his path.

In a battle that followed, the sheriff and many of his soldiers were killed.

On the strength of their victory Granuaile, her family and followers, together with the Bourkes and other Mayo clans, rose in all-out rebellion in a final attempt to get rid of Bingham.

They were soon joined by the O'Flahertys of Iar-Chonnacht, including Granuaile's second son, Murrough O'Flaherty, now chieftain of Ballinahinch.

Soon the west of Ireland was in arms. The Bourkes and the

O'Flahertys burned and raided the countryside right up to the gates of Galway city.

By sea Granuaile attacked the Aran Islands which had been recently given to an English planter.

Bingham could do little to stop her. He reported her raids to the English government and described her as 'the nurse to all rebellions in Connaught for 40 years'.

But the English government were growing fearful. They knew that if the rebellion spread, their army in Ireland was not strong enough to defeat it.

They removed Bingham from office and ordered him to remain in Athlone Castle.

The lord deputy came down from Dublin. He invited the rebel leaders to meet him for a peace conference in Galway.

Bingham was furious. 'Truly I have never heard the like of it between a prince and her subjects,' he complained angrily to London, 'much less with a race of such beggarly wretches as these ... This dalliance with these rebels,' he warned, 'makes them more insolent ... Without the sword ... it is impossible to govern the Irish.'

But the conference went ahead regardless of Bingham's objections.

Fearing a trap, the Gaelic chieftains refused to go into Galway city. The negotiations instead took place in open land outside the city walls.

The chieftains presented the lord deputy with a book of complaints about Bingham. They demanded that he be removed forever as governor of Connaught.

Among the complaints about Bingham and his relations was that they were responsible for killing Granuaile's son Owen O'Flaherty and also her Bourke nephews.

The chieftains also demanded that the old MacWilliam title should be conferred on the claimant by right of Brehon Law. This was William Bourke, Richard-in-Iron's brother.

But the negotiations were no more than a smokescreen. The chieftains were only biding their time, awaiting the return of Granuaile, who had sailed to Scotland for the gallowglass.

The negotiations eventually broke down.

When seven of Granuaile's galleys arrived in Erris in north Mayo, full of gallowglasses, the fighting resumed once again.

Chapter 15

BINGHAM RETURNS

With the additional forces brought in by Granuaile, the Bourkes pressed home their advantage against the English.

They recaptured Lough Mask Castle, chief castle of the MacWilliam, and plundered the country to the borders of Galway.

With Lough Mask Castle in their hands, they decided to restore the ancient MacWilliam title, outlawed by the English.

At a great assembley of all the Bourkes of Mayo at the traditional inauguration site of Rousakeera, William Bourke, Granuaile's brother-in-law, was elected the new MacWilliam. The rebellion now had an official figurehead.

As the rebellion spread, Queen Elizabeth's patience ran out. She ordered the lord deputy in Dublin to find Sir Richard Bingham either guilty or not guilty of the charges brought against him by the Bourkes.

In spring 1590, after a trial in Dublin, Bingham was found not guilty of the charges.

He was allowed back to Connaught to bring the rebellion to an end, by whatever means he chose. The means, as ever, was the sword.

With an army numbering over 1,000 soldiers, Bingham marched into Mayo. He captured Castlebar and then set out against the Bourkes who had assembled their forces in Tirawley.

The Bourkes, in the traditional Gaelic way of fighting, shadowed Bingham's progress from the protection of the woods and bogs. Then they made a sudden attack.

In the skirmish that followed, the MacWilliam was injured. His followers rushed him away and hid him on an island in Lough Conn. His injury was so serious that one of his legs had to be amputated.

By Gaelic law his disability made him unfit to continue as the MacWilliam and he had to resign from the chieftaincy.

Bingham pressed home the advantage and marched into Erris, killing and plundering as he went. The people fled before him into the mountains and woodlands. Bingham and his soldiers looted everything in their path and swept the countryside clean of live-stock and crops.

He then doubled back to attack Granuaile.

Chapter 16

MOTHER KNOWS BEST

Granuaile and her followers fled before Bingham to the safety of the islands in Clew Bay. For lack of ships, Bingham was unable to pursue them.

Instead, he took his anger out on the people left behind.

In his report to London, he boasted of how he 'slew all their woman and children'. Granuaile could hear their cries and the sound of the slaughter across the bay.

In the face of such a massacre, the rebellion began to crumble. Some of the Bourkes' allies submitted to Bingham on promise of their lives.

Granuaile, her son Tibóid and her Bourke nephews and in-laws continued to fight on. Bingham plundered her castle of Carraigahowley, stole her cattle and horses and lay waste to the countryside around.

The sea and her ships were now the only way Granuaile could provide for her family and followers. She swooped again on the Aran Islands and plundered the property of the new English owners.

Granuaile's men driving off her son's cattle.

Then news was brought to her that her second son, Murrough O'Flaherty of Ballinahinch, had allied with Bingham. Her anger knew no bounds. She decided to teach her son a lesson he would never forget for siding with her bitter enemy.

Granuaile set sail for Ballinahinch and made landfall at Murrough's castle of Bunowen. She ordered her men to burn and plunder the castle and drive off her son's cattle. Some of Murrough's soldiers, who were defending the castle, were killed in the attack.

It was a severe lesson to have to teach her son. But it worked. Murrough never crossed his mother again.

Chapter 17

BACK TO THE WALL

By 1592 most of the senior leaders of the Bourkes of Mayo had been killed in the war with Bingham.

Granuaile's youngest son, Tibóid, began to emerge as their new leader. He was married to Maeve O'Connor, sister of Donogh O'Connor, chieftain of Sligo.

Like the Gaelic chieftains elsewhere in the country at this time, Granuaile and the Bourkes were merely fighting their own corner. Their sole ambition was to protect their lands and property and preserve the rights they enjoyed under Brehon Law.

If the Gaelic chiefs had united under one single leader they could have defeated the English.

But the Gaelic chiefs often hated each other more than they did the English. That was their greatest weakness and the English were more than happy to take advantage of it.

Ireland was still divided into many chieftainships and lordships. There simply was no one leader powerful or strong enough to unite and lead all the chieftains under one banner.

An uneasy peace had descended on Connaught. Although Bingham had robbed her of her cattle and horse herds and had plundered her land, Granuaile still had her ships.

With them, she now had to feed and provide for her family and followers who depended on her. Like her ancestors before her, the sea provided her with the means of survival.

But the sea also gave her freedom and kept her out of Bingham's reach.

That is until an ill-planned attack by her son Tibóid put her freedom and safety in jeopardy once more.

Red Hugh O'Donnell, the son of the chieftain of Donegal, escaped from Dublin Castle in 1591. To stop his father rebelling against them, the English had captured Red Hugh and thrown him into prison. Red Hugh started plotting with Spain against England. To keep the English from finding out what he was doing, he needed a diversion.

In the spring of 1592 he persuaded Granuaile's son Tibóid to attack Bingham in Connaught. O'Donnell promised Tibóid more than he could give, including help from Spain.

On the strength of O'Donnell's promise, Tibóid started a rebellion in Mayo and attacked Bingham at Cloonagashel Castle.

The attack was unsuccessful and Tibóid's army was driven away. O'Donnell had failed to deliver on his promise of help.

Bingham was furious and sought revenge. He came with an army into Tibóid's territory of Burrishoole, near Granuaile's home.

The countryside around was only beginning to recover from the effects of the previous rebellion. Bingham stripped it bare of crops and cattle once more.

But this time Bingham did not stop with the land. English warships sailed into Granuaile's sea territory of Clew Bay and captured her fleet.

For the first time the secrets of Granuaile's sea empire were revealed: the network of islands, channels, the hidden reefs and shallows, the sheltered harbours that had protected her for decades, had now been uncovered by Bingham's ships.

No longer could her ships run before the wind on missions of trade or plunder or bring in the gallowglass from Scotland. No longer were they safe from pursuit in Clew Bay.

This was the greatest blow to Granuaile's freedom and to her power. Up until then, whatever happened on land, she knew she could always fall back on the sea. It is no wonder that she was furious with her son.

Chapter 18

LETTER TO A QUEEN

Bingham was delighted with the success of his mission against the woman who, from the very beginning of his reign as governor, had been the greatest obstacle to his efforts to conquer Connaught.

With much satisfaction he wrote to the English court, boasting of how he had penetrated Granuaile's sea domain and made her powerless.

But Granuaile was not someone who took such a setback lying down. And especially so when it came from her hated enemy Bingham.

Now, at the age of 63, in her stout castle at Carraigahowley, her lands devastated, her cattle herds taken, her people starving, English warships patrolling her sea domain, she was already plotting her next move.

And what a crafty move it proved to be.

In the bitter game played between herself and Bingham, the dice so far had fallen badly for Granuaile. Bingham was master of Mayo. She knew there was no way she could get the better of him in Ireland.

To get rid of him, she decided to go over his head to his boss, Queen Elizabeth I. It was a gamble but she had little left to lose.

In the Spring of 1593 she wrote her first letter to the queen.

Aware that Bingham had already blackened her name at the English court, Granuaile knew she had to present her case to Elizabeth and her shrewd ministers, especially her secretary of state, Lord Burghley, with great care and cunning, carefully choosing the right words.

Granuaile's letters show her to be politically astute and very shrewd.

In her letter to the queen she gave her version of the past events.

She tells Elizabeth that it was Bingham's harsh treatment of herself and her family that forced her to 'take arms and by force to maintain herself and her people by sea and by land the space of 40 years ...'

She knew that her part in past rebellions had been reported to the queen. She also realised that, as a result, her lands and those of her sons and her followers could, by English law, be confiscated.

Granuaile had to find a way to save her family's lands from falling into the hands of English planters and the English queen was the only person who could stop them.

Granuaile writing to Queen Elizabeth I.

To get around the charge of rebellion, she told the Queen that Bingham had forced her to rebel as the only way left to her to protect her people. Any plundering she had done by sea was simply to provide for them, as Bingham had taken their cattle and destroyed their crops.

Then, as a way to get back to sea, she asked the queen to give her 'free liberty during her life to invade with fire and sword all Your Highness' enemies ... without any interruption of any person whatsoever'. The person she had most in mind was Bingham.

It was an ingenious plan. In the guise of fighting for the queen, she could get the better of the queen's governor and continue her life at sea, free from Bingham's control.

She also asked for compensation for the damage done to her land and for the fortune in horses and cattle that Bingham had stolen from her.

Knowing that she and the queen were the same age, Granuaile played the sympathy vote and asked the queen to take into consideration her 'great age' and the 'little time she had to live'.

While her letter made its way to the English court though, something happened that added new urgency to her requests and which made Granuaile embark on the most dangerous voyage of her life.

Chapter 19

A DARING PLAN

Spurred on by their success over the chiefs in Connaught, in 1593 the English began to knock on the doors of Ulster, the last stronghold of Gaelic power.

Fearing that the English would overrun Ulster, as they had done in Connaught, two of the most powerful chieftains, Hugh O'Neill, chief of Tyrone, and Red Hugh O'Donnell, chief of Tirconail, agreed to put past differences behind them and unite to defend their lands. They sent a letter to the king of Spain to seek his help against the English.

The English, meanwhile, began to move against Ulster. The whole of Monaghan was declared Crown property and its chieftain, MacMahon, was executed.

They next moved against Maguire of Fermanagh, while Bingham looted and burned the lordship of O'Rourke of Breffni.

During the attack on O'Rourke, Bingham claimed he had intercepted a letter from Granuaile's son, Tibóid, implicating him in a plot to raise a new rebellion in Mayo.

Bingham arrested Tibóid, imprisoned him in the high-security castle of Athlone and charged him with treason. This was a crime punishable by death.

Whether Tibóid wrote such a letter or not, there is no proof. What is certain is that this was the very chance Bingham had been hoping for, to be rid of a troublesome chieftain and to strike another blow against Granuaile.

Granuaile realised there was not a moment to be lost if she was to save her son's life. Bingham's hatred of herself and her family spurred her into action.

She decided to follow her letter to the English court and to try and meet personally with the Queen.

The risks she undertook were enormous. While the sea journey to London was well within Granuaile's sailing ability, there were other dangers and uncertainties.

The seas around the west and south coasts of Ireland were now patrolled by English warships. A ship captained by such a notorious rebel and pirate would be considered a great prize by any English captain. Granuaile would be hanged from the ship's bow.

When she landed on English soil, would she not be immediately thrown into the Tower of London as a traitor and executed on the same charge of treason that now also hung over the head of her son?

Even if she did succeed in evading capture, how was she to get an audience with the queen of England?

Like Royalty and heads of state today, there were strict procedures and protocol involved. Few people were allowed an audience with the queen and, given her reputation, Granuaile's chances were slimmer than most.

But Granuaile was intelligent as well as bold. She knew that only someone close to the queen, someone she liked, someone with influence, could get her an audience. And she knew the very person.

Black Tom Butler, the earl of Ormond in Munster, was a relation and a favourite of Queen Elizabeth. Handsome and charming, he divided his time between the court and his estates in Ireland. The queen jokingly referred to him as 'her Black husband'.

But Granuaile also knew Black Tom through the longstanding connection of his ancestors with the lordship of Umhall.

She asked the earl for a letter of introduction to the queen's secretary of state, Lord Burghley. Black Tom agreed.

Armed with this and with a belief in her own powers of negotiation and persuasion, as well as her extraordinary stamina and courage, in June 1593 Granuaile set sail from Clew Bay on the most important voyage of her life.

Chapter 20

INTO THE LION'S DEN

Bingham's spies brought him news of Granuaile's departure to England.

He was furious that she had slipped through his fingers. But he was also worried what Granuaile might say about him, if she managed to get to see the queen.

He speedily wrote to remind the queen of all the trouble Granuaile had caused her by land and sea for 40 years. She was a traitor and a pirate and he had, he wrote, enough proof against her 'to hang her by justice'.

Meanwhile, Granuaile's galley sailed on its way down along the west coast, past Mizen Head and onwards towards the south coast of England. Past the Isles of Scilly, through the English Channel, into the Straits of Dover, it finally entered the Thames estuary.

On board, as well as her crew, Granuaile had brought some of her relations to act as her bodyguards, including her grand-nephew, Tibóid Reagh Bourke, who, it was later recorded, 'attended her at court'.

As her galley sailed up the great river towards the city of London, Granuaile entered a world very different from her home in the west of Ireland.

The River Thames teemed with traffic. Barges, lighters and the traditional Thames 'wherries' – small boats with a single sail – ferried cargo and passengers up and down that great water highway.

London was one of the busiest and wealthiest ports in the world. Along the bustling waterfront, trading ships from all over the known world – from Antwerp, Hamburg, Bordeaux, Venice and the Levant – discharged their cargoes of wine, spices, silk, carpets, metalwork, pottery, glass, pitch and timber and were loaded with the produce of England: tin, corn, coal and the woven cloth for which England was famous.

As her galley sailed further upriver, Granuaile saw for herself the royal palaces of Elizabeth – Greenwich, Whitehall and Westminster – and the mansions of the wealthy aristocracy and merchants, rising up from the river's edge.

But she also saw a sight which must have made her realise the terrible risk she took in sailing into the lion's den.

Along the riverbank she saw the rotting corpses of pirates who had paid the ultimate price for their crimes by being hung up in iron cages. It was a fate she knew could yet be hers.

She anchored her galley at one of the many landing stages below London Bridge and set foot in the great city of London.

Through the narrow streets and lanes, bordered on each side by wooden-framed houses, shops and taverns, Granuaile jostled her way through the constant mass of people: tradesmen selling their wares, porters carrying their loads, drovers driving herds of cattle, sheep and pigs, vying for space with pickpockets, beggars and sword-swinging young nobles spoiling for a fight, richly dressed ladies, their perfumed handkerchiefs held at the ready to stifle the awful smell of the open sewers, as they flitted from goldsmith to haberdasher.

All was noise, stench and movement, a far cry from the tranquillity and fresh air of Granuaile's home on the western coast of Ireland.

And whether she liked it or not, she would have to stay in this strange city until she achieved what she had come for.

It would take longer than she perhaps thought.

Chapter 21

EIGHTEEN QUESTIONS

Despite her letter of introduction from the earl of Ormond, Granuaile did not get to see the queen of England immediately.

Hundreds of people wanted an audience with the queen, many of them her own subjects, but very few succeeded. For someone from Ireland, a rebel and a pirate to boot, it was even more difficult.

For those lucky enough to be allowed into the queen's presence, certain procedures had to be gone through.

The queen's secretary of state, Lord Burghley, had read the letter Granuaile had sent to the queen. He was intrigued by her and what she wrote.

He already knew a lot about her from Sir Henry Sidney, Sir William Drury, Sir John Perrot and more lately from Bingham. But he wanted to find out more about her for himself.

He sent Granuaile a list of eighteen questions. They ranged from questions about her mother and father, her husbands and her children, to questions about the laws and customs of Ireland in relation to women, their dowries and inheritance.

He also asked her about the ownership of various lands and castles in Mayo and about the property owned by her relations and neighbours.

Granuaile knew she would have to be careful how she answered the questions.

If she answered them falsely, she might never get to meet the queen and her son would die. If she answered them truthfully, especially in relation to the questions about lands and property, she could provide the English with information that they could use against her family and neighbours.

Granuaile's answers are preserved to this day in the Elizabethan State Papers with notes in the margin in Lord Burghley's own handwriting.

Granuaile told him about her family, her mother, father, husbands and children and especially about the death of her eldest son, Owen, at the hands of Bingham and his relations.

She gave an account of her life – or the bits of it she knew would be less damaging in her quest to meet the queen – up to the death of her husband Richard.

She told Burghley of the harsh treatment she had received as a widow at the hands of Bingham; how he stole her cattle and horses, threw her into prison and built a gallows on which to hang her.

To Burghley's questions regarding specific castles and lands, because he misspelled their Gaelic names, she pretended that she had no knowledge of such places.

Granuaile waited in London while Lord Burghley studied her replies.

The waiting was a terrible time for her. If her answers were not acceptable she could still be thrown into prison. She had no idea if her son was still alive in Ireland or if Bingham had already executed him.

Then, in late July 1593, she received the news she had prayed for. The queen would see her at her palace of Greenwich.

Chapter 22

GOOD QUEEN BESS

A few miles from the city of London, Greenwich Palace looked out over the Thames.

It was Queen Elizabeth's favourite palace, especially in summertime, when the dirt and smells of London became too much and too dangerous for her health.

Elizabeth, known to her people as Good Queen Bess, was much-loved by them. By 1593 she had been on the throne for 35 years. During her reign, England had been peaceful and prosperous.

Her people looked on her as a goddess, their saviour from the Spanish invasion. For years she had steered her country safely through many dangers.

She had proved her critics wrong when they said that a woman on the throne would bring only misfortune to England. She had proved, as she said herself, that although she was a woman she had 'the heart and stomach of a king'.

Poets wrote sonnets and poems about her and the people cheered her wherever she went.

Elizabeth had never married. She feared that if she married a foreign prince or king, her husband would rule England instead of herself. If she married an English lord, it could divide her people and lead to a civil war.

'I will have but one mistress and no master,' she once said to the earl of Leicester, who wanted to marry her.

She had decided early in her life to sacrifice her own chance of happiness and of having children to make sure that her kingdom remained at peace and free from foreign rule. If she married a foreign prince she knew that instead of herself her husband would rule England.

Elizabeth was a brilliant scholar and could write and speak many languages, including Latin. She loved music and dancing, was an expert horsewoman and enjoyed hunting.

While she often gave great banquets for her court and for visiting nobles and ambassadors, she ate and drank very little herself.

She was tight-fisted with money and did not like waste. To save expense, each year she went on state visits to the castles of her richest nobles, bringing all her court and servants with her, which amounted to many hundreds of people. The noble had to foot the bill for the honour of entertaining Elizabeth and her court.

She loved to dress in magnificent gowns and dresses encrusted with rare gems, but there was a reason, other than fashion, for this display.

By her appearance Elizabeth created the image of a divine and untouchable goddess in the minds of her people and particularly in the minds of her nobles, in case they harboured any ideas of getting rid of her. She strutted through her court dressed like an exotic, tropical bird.

Elizabeth had a hot temper to match her flame-coloured hair. She was given to swearing and boxed the ears of her nobles when they displeased her.

She could be bad mannered, often spat and picked her teeth. She could also be very witty and had a razor-sharp tongue, which made many a nobleman quake in his boots before her.

Granuaile and Elizabeth were in many respects 'birds of a feather', being powerful women in what was, at that time, considered very much a man's world.

It was perhaps fitting that they should come face to face.

Chapter 23

THE MEETING

On a summer's day in July 1593, Granuaile's galley tied up at the landing stage near Greenwich Palace. It had been a long wait but the moment she had hoped and prayed for was now at hand.

Granuaile and her party were escorted through the long corridors of the palace, past large rooms, panelled in rich mahogany with tapestry-covered walls, sweeping staircases and galleries with high ceilings, decorated with intricate plasterwork.

It was a far cry from the simple surroundings of her stone castle at Carraigahowley.

Granuaile realised the difficult task that lay before her. There was no turning back. When she left Greenwich it would be as a prisoner or as a free woman.

She well knew that Bingham had blackened her name. Now, to save the life of her son, Granuaile would have to convince the queen to go against the advice of her own governor.

The fashionable courtiers and their ladies stared in wonderment as the elderly woman, bareheaded, her long, greying hair bound up in a knot, her face lined and weather-beaten by the wind and the salt spray, dressed in a woollen cloak that stretched to the ground, was lead past them towards the queen's private chamber.

While they tittered at her out-of-fashion clothes, something about her, the way she marched through the room, the look she may have thrown at them, made them realise they were in the presence of someone special, someone who, as a poet wrote of her, was

> ... well used to power, as one that hath
> Dominion over men of savage mood
> And dared the tempest in its midnight wrath
> And thru' opposing billows cleft her fearless path.

They looked at her in awe.

This, after all, was the notorious woman pirate from the far west of Ireland they had heard about from Sir Philip Sidney – commander of rebels and pirates, the scourge of English merchant ships.

What on earth was the queen thinking about to agree to see such a woman?

As the doors of the presence chamber closed behind her, Granuaile came face to face with the woman against whom she had rebelled and in whose hands her life and her son's life now lay; the very woman whose servants in Ireland had turned Granuaile's world upside down.

Granuaile saw a woman about the same age as herself, but there the resemblance ended.

The queen was dressed in a richly embroidered gown, studded with diamonds and precious gems, which dazzled and shone in the sunlight.

Behind the mask of the magnificent dress and fabulous gems, Granuaile saw that the queen's face was like a mask, covered in white rice powder and rouge. Her nose was hooked and her teeth were black. Her head was covered in a red wig.

Elizabeth peered short-sightedly at the 'notorious rebel', the 'famous feminine sea-captain', about whom her ministers in Ireland had written. She saw standing before a woman about her own age, dressed plainly, no paint or powder to hide her wrinkled face.

But something about the way the Irishwoman stood, as if they were equals instead of queen and subject, made Elizabeth realise she was looking at someone special. This woman did not need fine dresses or gems to mark her out as being a leader.

Despite her titles of High Admiral of her navy and Chief Commander of her armies, Elizabeth knew that, unlike this woman who stood before her, she had done little to deserve them.

Unlike Granuaile, she had never led her troops into battle or sailed

Granuaile with Queen Elizabeth I.

further downriver than Greenwich. Her titles were empty. Granuaile's were the real thing.

It was said that the two women spoke to each other in Latin. The queen spoke many languages, but Granuaile could also speak English and knew some Spanish as well.

The queen was curious to hear directly from Granuaile about her strange life on land and sea. Was it true she had led rebellions? Had she plundered English ships at sea? The queen peered at the document on the table beside her and pointed in disbelief to a particular sentence. Was it true that she had even attacked her own son?

Taking a deep breath, Granuaile knew that she must be careful how she answered Elizabeth. She had to choose her words with care.

Granuaile told the Queen she had no option but had been forced to take action to protect herself, her family and her followers because of the disturbed state of her country.

She explained Connaught was in such a state, where the people were terrified, the countryside devastated, due to the actions of the queen's own servants there, especially Bingham. Instead of justice, Bingham had brought only grief to her and her people.

The queen listened with growing admiration and pity as Granuaile told her how she and her family had suffered at Bingham's hands and of his 'hard dealing' of herself, in particular.

She asked that her son be released from prison. The queen said she would consider it and promised Granuaile that in the meantime her son should come to no harm while in Bingham's custody.

Then Granuaile played her trump card.

She needed desperately to return to the sea in order to recoup her losses on land. But to do this she had to get Bingham off her back. The only way around him was if she could get the queen's specific permission.

Referring to her seafaring activities as 'maintenance by land and sea' – which sounded more law-abiding than piracy and plunder – she asked Elizabeth to allow her to return to her seafaring ways. Elizabeth agreed. Granuaile led her to believe that, as the queen wrote, by doing so she would be 'fighting Our quarrel with all the world'.

Granuaile had pulled a fast one. She could return to her former trade by sea, this time with the queen's permission, and there was nothing Bingham could do to stop her.

The queen wrote her orders in a letter to Bingham. Ignoring the accusations he had made against Granuaile, she ordered him to release Tibóid and, in future, to allow him and his half-brother, Murrough O'Flaherty, to 'live in peace and enjoy their livelihoods'.

She urged him to 'have pity on this aged woman' and to ensure that she be allowed 'maintenance' for the 'rest of her old years'.

With much thanks and vague promises of loyalty, Granuaile took her leave of the queen, her mission a success.

Such was the impact Granuaile made on the queen and her court that when Elizabeth I was having a new map of Ireland drawn by her mapmaker, Baptista Boazio, later that year, Granuaile's name was included as chieftain of Mayo. She was the only woman whose name had ever appeared on a map of a country.

It was proof that regardless of law and custom, Granuaile had, by her sheer ability and courage, become accepted as a chieftain in her own right, both in Ireland and England.

Armed with the queen's letter, Granuaile set sail for Ireland and was home in Clew Bay in September.

Chapter 24

BINGHAM'S REVENGE

On her return, Granuaile confronted Bingham with the queen's letter. She demanded that he release Tibóid immediately and give her back her ships.

Bingham was furious. He realised that Granuaile had pulled the wool over the queen's eyes. She had played the part of the much-wronged, old woman well at court.

Despite everything he had done to defeat this terrible woman, here was his own queen undoing all his hard work and allowing Granuaile to return to her plundering ways while pretending to be loyal to the queen.

He well knew the trouble Granuaile was still capable of causing. He ignored the queen's orders as long as he dared.

Granuaile threatened that she would return to court and report his insubordination.

Eventually Bingham knew he had no alternative but to agree to her demands. He released Tibóid in November.

Tibóid had suffered greatly while in prison. He had been tortured so badly, he could barely stand.

Once Tibóid was safely out of Bingham's clutches, Granuaile prepared to return to sea. She started to build new galleys.

But Bingham vowed to stop her. Just as her galleys were ready to sail in the spring of 1594, he pounced.

He stationed a troop of soldiers beside her castle and ordered them to accompany Granuaile on every sea trip she made.

Granuaile realised the game was up. With English soldiers tailing her ships there was little she could do. Despite all the queen's power, Bingham was still master in Mayo.

Soon food began to run out as Bingham's soldiers once again plundered the land around Clew Bay, leaving it bare.

With starvation staring her and her followers in the face, Granuaile knew she had to take action.

In March 1595, under cover of darkness, with her family and crew, her galley stole out of Clew Bay and headed south.

Granuaile sailed along the Munster coast until she reached Carrick-on-Suir, home of Black Tom, the earl of Ormond.

There, in his newly-built Elizabethan manor house, Granuaile told the powerful earl how Bingham had disobeyed the queen's orders.

With Black Tom's help, she wrote again to Lord Burghley.

She told him of the treatment she had received since her return from court. She also claimed that Sir Richard Bingham had tried to have her killed.

It was Granuaile's intention to go straight to London from Carrick-on-Suir to present her letter in person to Lord Burghley. The earl of Ormond even wrote her another letter of introduction.

But before she could set sail for London, political events in another part of Ireland intervened.

Chapter 25

THE SHOWDOWN

In the summer of 1595, the Ulster chieftains Hugh O'Neill and Red Hugh O'Donnell went into open rebellion against Elizabeth.

They wrote letters to the King of Spain offering him the 'Crown of Ireland' if he helped them to get rid of the English.

The rebellion was mainly confined to parts of Ulster. Many Gaelic chieftains feared O'Neill and O'Donnell as much as they feared the English, but in the coming war they would be forced to take sides.

To stop the rebellion spreading to other parts of Ireland, the queen ordered her officials to back off from terrorising chieftains like Granuaile and her sons.

She had Bingham removed as governor of Connaught and on his return to England he was thrown into prison.

A new governor of Connaught, Sir Conyers Clifford, was appointed in his place.

With her greatest enemy out of the picture, it was not long before Granuaile was back on the sea.

Her ships were sighted off the coast of Clare as she led a plundering mission on the lands of the earl of Thomond.

In 1596, at the age of 66, Granuaile sailed to Scotland to lead an attack on MacNeill, chief of Barra, because he had raided her lands in Mayo.

As the war between the Ulster chieftains and the English intensified, both sides recognised the importance of Granuaile's sea power. There were no other galleys in Ireland at the time.

At first she and her two sons sided with the Ulster chieftains.

Towards the end of 1596, however, a feud erupted between the Mayo Bourkes and Red Hugh O'Donnell, which forced Granuaile, her son and most of her Bourke relations to change sides from O'Donnell to the English.

This was not the first time that a feud had occurred between the O'Donnells and the Bourkes. There had been bad blood between the two clans for many generations. More recently O'Donnell had failed in his promise to support Tibóid in his attack on Bingham.

To show the Bourkes who was boss, Red Hugh O'Donnell raided and plundered Mayo. Against Brehon Law, as well as the wishes of the Bourkes, he tried to force them to accept a MacWilliam chosen by him.

Granuaile on her galley.

Granuaile's son Tibóid, the strongest Bourke leader, was having none of it. He refused to accept O'Donnell's MacWilliam and ran him out of Mayo.

O'Donnell hit back at Tibóid. He captured him, took him as a prisoner to Tirconail and raided his territory around Clew Bay. Granuaile was powerless to stop him.

Tibóid escaped and returned to Mayo. He found that O'Donnell had devastated his lands and that of his relations. Famine again stalked Mayo and the people were on the verge of starvation.

Granuaile and Tibóid were forced to live on board their ships.

The English governor, Clifford, was also anxious to have Granuaile and her son as allies in the war between the English and the Ulster chieftains. He offered them a deal.

Caught in a trap between both sides, in August 1597 Granuaile, Tibóid and most of their Bourke, O'Malley and O'Flaherty relations agreed to the terms Clifford offered.

Tibóid was to be granted most of the lands of the MacWilliam in Mayo. He would continue as leader of his mother's army and ships and was given enough money to re-stock his lands and feed his people.

With O'Donnell still snapping at their heels they had little option but to agree.

Hugh O'Neill later tried to patch up the quarrel between O'Donnell and Granuaile and Tibóid. He too realised how important their influence, as well as their sea-power, would be in the war against the English.

But by then it was too late.

Inter-clan feuding had once more proved to be the weakness of Gaelic unity. It was now every chieftain for himself.

Chapter 26

THE END OF AN ERA

Granuaile was now in her late sixties. Her seafaring days were coming to a close.

Old and weary, she lived out her last years in the frugal comfort of her stout fortress of Carraigahowley. By this time she had handed over control of her army and her ships to her son Tibóid.

Despite the agreement he had made with the English, Tibóid continued to put his and his clan's needs first during the nine years' war between the Ulster chieftains and the English.

Like many other chieftains, he changed sides with the ebb and flow of events, as one side got the upper hand of the other, in the long-drawn out war, before the final battle of Kinsale in 1601.

At Kinsale, with 3,000 of his fellow countrymen, including his half-brother, Murrough O'Flaherty, Tibóid eventually fought with the English against his old enemy O'Donnell.

What Granuaile thought about her sons and her relations fighting with the English we do not know.

What we do know, however, is that we cannot judge their actions by standards that do not apply to the times they lived in, or to the situation they found themselves in.

The sixteenth century was, above all else, a time of survival. There was no 'United Ireland' to fight for. Each chieftain saw it as his only duty as to protect himself, his clan and his land. His loyalty was to his clan, not to his country.

Many chieftains still preferred to fight against their neighbours, rather than unite against the English. Many, like Hugh O'Donnell and the Bourkes, harboured ancient grudges which turned some chieftains, like Tibóid, against them.

Granuaile lived to hear of the defeat of O'Neill and O'Donnell at Kinsale. She perhaps also realised that more than just a battle had been lost there.

Kinsale brought the curtain down on the old Gaelic way of life into which Granuaile had been born and reared. It signalled the end of an ancient lifestyle and the world of clans, chieftains and gallowglass, a world that had not moved with the times and had been left behind by the rest of the world.

After Kinsale a new political age dawned in which both her sons prospered. Both had chosen the winning side.

But it was also an age that had no place for a warrior woman like Granuaile.

She died in 1603, the same year as Queen Elizabeth I.

Alike in character, and in their role as leaders in a man's world, each represented a culture that had little in common. When these cultures collided, there could only be one winner.

Granuaile is buried in the little abbey church on Clare Island, looking out on the Atlantic, a fitting resting place for a sea queen.

Over the centuries her memory has been kept alive in folklore, legend, poetry and song.

Today she has, at last, become part of Ireland's history too.

Chapter 27

GRANUAILE'S DESCENDANTS

Granuaile's youngest son, Tibóid, survived the battle of Kinsale and returned to Mayo.

He lived and prospered under the new English system of government which after Kinsale gradually replaced the old Brehon system of his ancestors.

In the early years of the new century, Tibóid left his seafaring days behind him. He moved inland from Clew Bay to the lands around Lough Mask which once had been part of his father's MacWilliam estate.

He lived at nearby Kinturk Castle, which he inherited from his foster-father, Myles MacEvilly. He also owned Kilboynell Castle which was subsequently renamed Castle Bourke. He received a knighthood from Queen Elizabeth's successor, James I, in 1603.

But Sir Tibóid continued to live more like a Gaelic chieftain than an English lord. He continued to be an influential figure in Connaught and represented County Mayo in the Parliament in Dublin.

By shrewd dealing and competing successfully against the wave of

English planters who descended on Connaught in the years after Kinsale, Tibóid became one of the few Gaelic chieftains to hold on to and even increase his estate.

This he did by being as cunning and able as those who wanted to take his land from him, and by adapting to the changed political and social circumstances in which he found himself.

At his death, he was the single largest landowner in Mayo, with an estate of over 60,000 acres of land.

In 1627 Tibóid was made the First Viscount Mayo by King Charles I. He died in 1629 and is buried in Ballintobber Abbey, County Mayo.

He had four sons and three daughters by his wife, Maeve O'Connor Sligo.

His eldest son, Myles, succeeded him to the title and to most of his estate, the rest of which he divided between his three other sons.

There were eight Viscounts Mayo before the title was made extinct around the turn of the nineteenth century.

Today, Granuaile's descendants, through her son Tibóid, are living in Westport House, County Mayo, built near the original O'Malley Castle of Cathair-na-Mart.

Granuaile's other surviving son, Murrough O'Flaherty, continued to live at Bunowen Castle in Connemara. He died in 1626 and was buried in the Abbey of St Francis in Galway city.

Her grandson, also named Murrough, was dispossessed of his lands by Cromwell.

His descendants lived on in Connemara for many generations, eventually becoming mere tenants of their former ancestral lands.

GRANUAILE – A TIMELINE

c. 1530   Born in the lordship of Umhall, County Mayo, daughter of chieftain Owen (Dubhdara) and Margaret O'Malley from whom she learned her seafaring expertise.

1546   Given in marriage to Donal of the Battles O'Flaherty, tanaiste of the clan O'Flaherty of Bunowen, in Connemara.

1547-1552   Gives birth to two sons, Owen and Murrough, and a daughter, Margaret.

1560   Donal killed in an inter-clan dispute. Grace avenges his death and assumes leadership of his clan on behalf of her sons.

1564   Returns to Umhall and settles on Clare Island from where she starts her career of 'maintenance by land and sea', with her father's ships and a private army of 200 men. Her fame as a leader and an expert mariner grows.

1565   Rescues Hugh de Lacy from the sea and they fall in love. She takes a terrible retribution on the MacMahons when they kill Hugh.

1566   When the English administration begins to push into Mayo, she marries Richard-in-Iron Bourke, whose castle, Rockfleet, is less exposed than Clare Island. When she has moved her ships and army into Richard's castle she divorces him.

1567	Her son Theobald (Tibóid-ne-Long) Toby-of-the-Ships is born aboard her ship. She defends her new-born son from an attack from Barbery Pirates. On her return to Rockfleet she becomes re-united with Richard-in-Iron.
1571	With Grace's help, Richard-in-Iron becomes tanaiste (elected successor) to the MacWilliam of Mayo, the premier chiefdom in Mayo.
1576	The MacWilliam of Mayo submits to Queen Elizabeth of England. Richard-in-Iron's position as his successor is under threat.
1577	With her army and navy, Grace impresses Elizabeth's minister, Sir Henry Sidney in Galway with her power.
1577	Grace plunders the lands of Desmond and is captured by the Earl of Desmond, who imprisons her in Limerick Jail.
1578	To save his own neck, Desmond hands her over to the English Governor.
1578	Grace is thrown into the dungeons of Dublin Castle.
1579	Richard-in-Iron rises in rebellion. Grace is released from prison by the English.
1579	Grace plunders English ships. She routes an English army sent to beseige her at Rockfleet.

1580	The MacWilliam dies and his son succeeds him by English law. Grace and Richard go into the rebellion to secure their rights. Grace's ships bring in the infamous Scottish mercenaries, the Gallowglass. The English are no match for them and agree to deal. Richard becomes the MacWilliam of Mayo.
1581	Grace and Richard try and stop the English from taking their lands.
1583	Richard-in-Iron dies. Grace immediately takes Rockfleet Castle as her base.
1584	Sir Richard Bingham is appointed English Governor. He sets out to destroy Grace and her family.
1584	Grace leads a rebellion against Bingham.
1586	Bingham's brother kills Grace's eldest son, Owen.
1586	Under the guise of a truce, Bingham lures Grace to his headquarters. he proclaims her a traitor and condemns her to death. She is rescued by her son-in-law.
1587	Grace flees to Ulster to consult with O'Neill. With his ally, O'Donnell, he is plotting to unite the Irish for the first time and, with help from the king of Spain, to drive the English out of Ireland.
1588	The Spanish Armada is driven by bad weather to its doom. Bingham exacts revenge on Grace and her relations for helping the Spanish. They retaliate and Bingham declares all-out war.

1589	Bingham accuses Grace of treason and of being 'the nurse to all rebellions in Ireland' and reports her to Queen Elizabeth.
1590	Bingham pressurises Grace's second son, Murrough, to ally with him. Furious, Grace attacks Murrough.
1591	By adopting a 'scorched earth' tactic, Bingham finally defeats Grace.
1592	In desperation Grace writes to Elizabeth to complain about Bingham.
1593	Bingham seizes her youngest son Tibóid and charges him with treason, a crime punishable by death.
1593	Grace makes a momentous and dangerous decision. She will sail to London and put her case to Elizabeth face-to-face.
1593	She is successful. Against Bingham's advice Elizabeth grants Grace an audience at her glittering Court at Greenwich. Showing a shrewd negotiating ability and daring, Grace out-manouvers the Queen, secure her son's release and boldly elicits the Queen's permission to continue her career by land and sea.
1594	Bingham is recalled to England and Grace returns unhindered to her old career by sea.
1597	At the 'great age' of 67, Grace is still actively leading her men by sea. She attacks MacNeil of Barra off the Scottish coast.

1601	The Battle of Kinsale and the end of the Gaelic world of Grace O'Malley.
1603	Grace dies at Rockfleet.

FURTHER READING

Books

Chambers, Anne, *Granuaile: Ireland's Pirate Queen (Grace O'Malley)*, 1530-1603, Wolfhound/Merlin, 2003

Ellis, Steven, *Tudor Ireland*, Longman, 1985

MacCurtain, M. & O'Dowd, M., *Women in Early Modern Ireland*, Wolfhound Press, 1991

Stanley, J. *Bold in her Breeches*, Pandora, 1995

Videos

Pirate Queen, Radharc/RTE, 1985
Legends of the Isles, Learning Channel, USA, 1993
Warrior Women, Discovery Channel, Europe, 2004

Websites

Grace O'Malley – Official site – www.graceomalley-annechambers.com
Westport House – www.westporthouse.ie

INDEX